This book is dedicated to my angels,
written for and inspired by.

www.mascotbooks.com

Tuesday Bluesday

Officially licensed by the US Navy

For more information, please contact:
Mascot Books
620 Herndon Parkway #320
Herndon, VA 20170
info@mascotbooks.com

Library of Congress Control Number: 2018904808

CPSIA Code: PBANG0618A
ISBN-13: 978-1-68401-711-9

Printed in the United States

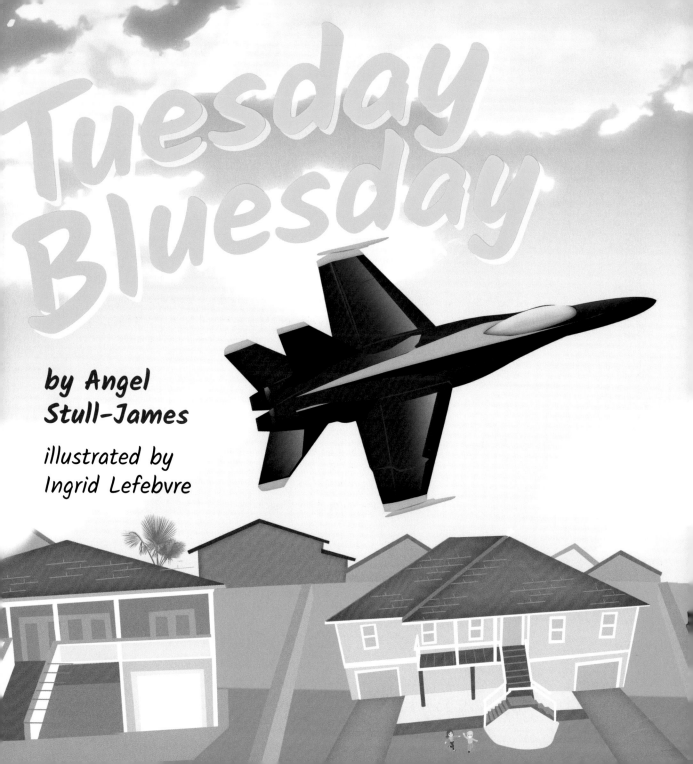

Tuesday Bluesday

by Angel Stull-James

illustrated by Ingrid Lefebvre

In the morning we wake
to an earthquake-like shake,

and a thunderous roar
zooms past our front door.

Adjusting to the morning light as we lay,

we think to ourselves it
must be Tuesday Bluesday.

As fast as we can, we run to the window, pointing up to the sky, watching them fly so very, very high.

We shout "Blues!"
as if they can hear,
for why wouldn't they?
They are so very near.

we love to watch our
Blue Angels soar.

Here come the solos
with heart-pounding rollovers.

They travel near,
and they travel far.
When they're home, locals
stop to watch from their cars.

Summertime on the beach is the big hometown show.
Miles of people line up in the sand, standing toe to toe.

Thousands of boats go go go,
and out of nowhere

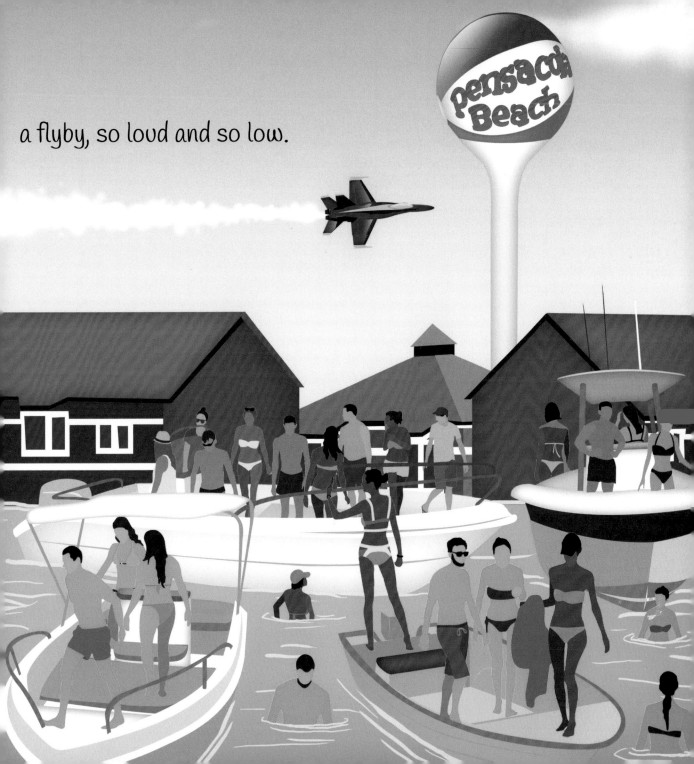

a flyby, so loud and so low.

Some only see the Blues once a year,

but we are privileged enough to watch them every week from our pier.

"Safe flying today, Blue Angels!" we say,

and we pray tomorrow will be another wonderful Bluesday.

Sweet dreams for now, snug in our beds,

for we know in the morning our
Angels will be flying overhead.

the
end

About the Author

Angel Stull-James is a native of Pensacola, Florida, and an honored graduate from Florida State University. Angel is a former child model and actress and worked in the fashion industry with numerous prominent design houses in New York City. She is a certified county mediator and licensed attorney in Florida and New York. After moving back home and working as in-house lead counsel for numerous years at a local firm, she decided to resign and focus on herself and her family. Angel is a mother of twins, who she says are her greatest accomplishment and her whole world! Angel has always enjoyed writing and was published at a young age, but it is her twins who have inspired her to follow her passion for writing and pursue it more thoroughly. She has since written numerous books for her twins.

Angel states, "*Tuesday Bluesday* is about Pensacola's hometown Blue Angels and my twins' experience and love for the Blues at such a young age. *Tuesday Bluesday* portrays the Blue Angels in a positive light and depicts the excitement of our community to have the Blue Angels in our lives. The book is fun and upbeat, and the rhymes are a fun read for children. Reading is such an important part of a child's life and to begin reading at a young age is crucial."

Have a book idea?

Contact us at:

info@mascotbooks.com | www.mascotbooks.com